OUT OF BAD COMES GOOD

THE ADVANTAGES OF DISADVANTAGES

JERRY DEL COLLIANO

NEW YORK

OUT OF BAD COMES GOOD
The Advantages of Disadvantages

by Jerry Del Colliano

ISBN 978-1-61448-016-7 (paperback)
ISBN 978-1-61448-017-4 (eBook)
Library of Congress Control Number: 2011926889

Published by:

MORGAN JAMES PUBLISHING
The Entrepreneurial Publisher
5 Penn Plaza, 23rd Floor
New York City, New York 10001
(212) 655-5470 Office
(516) 908-4496 Fax
www.MorganJamesPublishing.com

Cover Design by:
Rachel Lopez
rachel@r2cdesign.com

Interior Design by:
Bonnie Bushman
bbushman@bresnan.net

In an effort to support local communities, raise awareness and funds, Morgan James Publishing donates one percent of all book sales for the life of each book to Habitat for Humanity.
Get involved today, visit
www.HelpHabitatForHumanity.org.

DEDICATION

This book is dedicated to my family — my wife, Cheryl, the love of my life and the kindest person I have ever known and to whom I owe the happiness she brings me everyday. And my son, Jerry and daughter Daria. You are life's gift to me. The wisdom in this book is my eternal gift to you.

To my inspiration, mentor and friend, Father Martin Padovani who connected me to my spirituality by introducing me to myself.

And my dear friend, Morris "Jim" Weinraub. Hardly a day passes in which I do not miss his counsel, humor and outstanding human relations — much of which I have purloined here or as Jimmy would say — *"researched"*.

With sincere appreciation to A. Winfield "Wynn" Etter without whom my love, respect and devotion to the teachings of Dale Carnegie would have been missing from my life. Wynn is the most positive person I have ever known. His favorite saying -- *"none are so old as those who have outlived enthusiasm"* -- is my constant mantra.

To my mother, Adele who instilled in me the spirit to never give up and my father, Gerard, whose honesty set a standard that is hard to attain. I miss them both very much.

A special thanks to my students at The University of Southern California who inspired and encouraged me to write this book and to Bobi Seredich without whom it would have been impossible.

FOREWORD

Do you want to be inspired? Do you feel you are stuck in your life's journey? Do you feel you live in a culture of negativity? The refreshing and encouraging words and reflections by Jerry Del Colliano in *Out Of Bad Comes Good -- The Advantages of Disadvantages* might answer these questions. He will shed some insight in these and other troubled areas of your life.

Writing with conviction and compassion, Del Colliano will stimulate and energize us to confront our lagging spirits.

Anytime we can adjust and inspire our distorted perceptions of ourselves, others and situations, we will be able to cope better with life's problems. Wayne Dyer puts it quite simply, *"When we change the way we look at things, the things we look at will change."* Anytime we can cope better, we will gain more hope. Isn't this the basic message of Viktor Frankl whom Jerry quotes? *"When we have hope we can cope.* " The good results of all this is an emboldened self-confidence.

Taking personal responsibility for our lives; taking personal responsibility for our own happiness are two striking themes that are woven throughout the chapters. These two truths are so important for attaining emotional maturity and a good relationship with ourselves. Then we will have the tools to form healthy relationships with others.

Jerry intersperses throughout the book graphic examples and pertinent quotes from well-known persons who have struggled with their life's problems and failures but managed to bring good out of bad.

Del Colliano candidly reveals some of his own painful sufferings, mistakes and failures. With much effort and work, he found good, success and healing as he grew beyond his past failures and family of origin. Jesus said it so well; *"The truth will set you free."* However, He didn't say it wouldn't hurt.

His grateful attitude to God acknowledges and witnesses to God's presence in his life and his dependence on God, his Higher Power. At the same time, Jerry frequently reiterates his respect for others perception of God. On the other hand, his growth and struggle with his faith development was a choice he made.

I particularly like the chapters on Divorce and Shame, two issues that are very relevant for our times. Jerry experienced divorce but had the positive attitude that people can learn from divorce and become better persons. I can attest to that also many times over in my own counseling ministry. I also agree with Jerry, that good second marriages are possible if people learn how they failed in the first marriage.

There is a healthy shame that we all need – that we are worthwhile persons with boundaries and limitations. The "shamed" and the "shameless" are unfortunately present in epidemic proportions in society.

Out of Bad Comes Good — The Advantages of Disadvantages only verifies what the Good News of Jesus Christ proclaims. We can all change and be transformed. The question is – do we want to change and be healed?

Rev. Martin Padovani, M.S.
Individual, Marriage and
Family Therapist

IN A NUTSHELL

Every disadvantage in life comes
with one or more advantages.

To live life to the fullest, deal with your problems,
use your God-given gifts and always remember
to be grateful for that which you have.

At the end of the day when you've done everything
you can, resignation and acceptance. Trust in God.

Go on a life long Jealousy Diet and relieve yourself
of the dead weight that kills relationships.

Shame kills self-esteem. Love of self kills shame.

Dream on, but keep your motivation high
and your expectations low.

Remarkably enough, simply thinking and
believing that you have an edge, gives you the edge.

The only average that counts is batting a 1.000 at trying.

When it comes to what gets into your psyche,
be in charge.

To paraphrase Bob Dylan, come to learn
that career "chaos is a friend of mine".

Out of bad marriages come good people who,
when they commit to dealing with their family of
origin issues, can then enter into healthy relationships.

Reach for a Higher Power when your faith is low.

Good happens anyway. Be prepared.

CONTENTS

1

THE ADVANTAGES
OF DISADVANTAGES

"When we are no longer able to change a situation –
we are challenged to change ourselves." – Viktor Frankl

I first saw the phrase "learn to appreciate the advantages of disadvantages" in a book written by Bishop Fulton J. Sheen, a charismatic Catholic clergyman who, believe it or not, actually did a weekly half-hour prime-time network television show about God and religion in the 1950's Golden Age of Television. Talk about a reality show!

The advantages of disadvantages – sounds like something your mother or father would say to you when your world is falling apart. "Don't worry, things will get better." My mother would say, "Every dog has its day" but we didn't have a dog and my day seemed like it would never come.

Life has not been easy.

My father had a heart attack when I was six years old. On that day I felt the burden of losing my childhood and eventually becoming the man of the house. I developed a nervous tick. Was so painfully shy my parents were called to school to deal with why I did not participate in class. Had surgery at 21 for a rare congenital stomach condition that causes a great deal of pain. I've been divorced twice. Fired from more than one media job – and although that is normal in broadcasting, it still hurts. Developed a profitable business and then one day the media company known as The Evil Empire, Clear Channel, sued my business for $100 million. They settled out of court to get me to drop my countersuit, but I was prohibited from working in radio for four years.

And it seems to never end.

Of course, my problems are the best problems for me to have. I've come to know now. And I can prove it.

When I worked for Dale Carnegie Training as an instructor, I often asked my classes to take a 3x5 card and write down their three biggest problems in no particular order. However, I asked them *not* to write their names on the card. When everyone completed the assignment, the class members passed the cards to the center aisle and they were collected. Then, I spread all the cards out on a table face down in the front of the classroom and asked each and every one in the room to come forward and randomly pick up a card and return to their seats.

An amazing thing happened.

After the class had a moment to look at someone else's three problems, not one person wanted to trade their troubles for someone else's. They wanted their *own* cards back with their *own* problems as bad as some of them were. I've conducted this exercise many times and have yet to find even one person who wanted to trade for another's problems. That was very powerful because it said that as bad as things can get for human beings, we'd just as soon keep the situations with which we are struggling.

It seems our entire world is focused on good fortune. And we spend a lot of time hoping for that *one* break, *one* moment, *one* thing that fulfills our dreams.

This book is not about waiting for good fortune. It is devoted to cultivating a way to deal with problems, use our life's skills while finding ways to be grateful for that which we have. Ever notice when someone wins the lottery and gets their dream of all dreams – lots of money and the freedom that it supposedly brings – that so many winners spend it all, lose their loved ones in the process and wind up worse off for their good luck? Broke in every way.

Evelyn Adams won the New Jersey lottery not once, but twice (in 1985 and 1986) for a total of $5.4 million all of which she spent. Today she lives in a trailer not a palatial home. William "Bud" Post won the Pennsylvania Lottery to the tune of $16.2 million in 1988. He said in interviews that he wished it never happened – imagine that! Wishing that he *never* won millions of dollars. Today, Post is reportedly living on social security and food stamps. It is not hard to find stories like these and I don't mean to dissuade you from playing the lottery for fun and profit. My point is that we don't only need good fortune to make us happy. Disadvantages can turn out to have advantages and seemingly good things can turn into bad.

When you finish reading this book, I hope you will see that there is always light at the end of the tunnel. That good routinely comes from bad and our job should be learning how to expect it because good is going to happen in spite of us. That's right. Bad things happen, but so do good things.

There is the moving story of Viktor Frankl, author of *Man's Search for Meaning* about his incarceration at a Nazi concentration camp in World War II.

Frankl, a psychiatrist, concluded that real meaning in life is discovered in every living moment. That life never stops having meaning even facing the suffering of the Holocaust and death.

This man, thrust in the worst of all unimaginable situations, came away from his captivity finding that his new wife was dead (taken and killed at a separate camp) but still optimistic that everyone who faces great problems has someone in their lives whether a Higher Power or a friend that must not be disappointed.

In the Wiki description of his excellent book, *"Frankl concludes from his experience that a prisoner's psychological reactions are not solely the result of the conditions of his life, but also from the freedom of choice he always has even in severe suffering. The inner hold a prisoner has on his spiritual self relies on having a faith in the future, and that once a prisoner loses that faith, he is doomed."*

Man's Search for Meaning is the single most uplifting book I have ever read in spite of its subject matter.

Nothing in my life and probably yours compares to the trials of Viktor Frankl, for sure.

But understanding that the advantages of disadvantages are a reassurance that life's hurts and obstacles can be overcome is monumental and that in the end new life's experiences arise.

Our mission, then, is to gain a new appreciation for the vicissitudes of life.

How to ride the roller coaster that most assuredly will go up and down – sometimes way up, and way down –

for everyone no matter who we are, where we live or how much money we have.

Cultivating a new way to deal with life's problems makes each painful experience transformative.

Every disadvantage in life comes with
one or more advantages.

2

THREE STEPS TO A MEANINGFUL LIFE

"When we are no longer able to change a situation, we are challenged to change ourselves" – that was said by Viktor Frankl in *Man's Search For Meaning* an outstanding and moving book about Frankl's time spent in World War II concentration camps.

Since problems aren't likely to go away, perhaps Frankl's advice also rings true for us – *change the way we face adversity.*

The obvious is not so obvious which is why I believe there are benefits to altering the way we look at things. We may be spending more time trying to change the circumstances surrounding our problems rather than look inward and try to change ourselves. As George Carlin said, *"I put a dollar in one of those change machines. Nothing changed."*

There are three things we need to do every day to make life more rewarding and worthwhile.

1. Don't solve problems, just deal with them

It is rare when most people can get through one single day without encountering a problem. Did I say "a" problem? Often, there are *many* problems that crop up and sometimes they occur almost simultaneously. What is an overwhelmed person to do? One revelation that most of us don't even consider is to *not* try to solve the problems that come our way.

That's right. Let me say that again. It's better to deal with a problem and work through it than it is to solve it immediately. There is a difference.

The human reaction when we are faced with adversity is to fix what is wrong. Therein lies problem number one. Some things just cannot get fixed right away. When Clear Channel sued my company for $100 million, believe me when I say I wanted *that* situation fixed right away. Unfortunately or fortunately, if you believe me, there was no need to resolve the lawsuit even though it brought me great stress and concern.

Over the years that elapsed, I learned to deal with the legal action that I didn't ask for. Eventually, I countersued and only months before all the litigation was scheduled for trial, the issues were settled and Clear Channel bought my company as we both agreed to drop our lawsuits. Who could have known this could be the favorable outcome when the original problem occurred? Who could have seen at first that the best solution would be the last solution?

Therefore, the message is deal with your problems – work through them. Don't deny that they exist. That's all that can be expected. After all, some problems go away – they rectify themselves with little or no help. Others cannot be resolved and therefore we must do the best we can to accept the outcome favorable or not. Then, of course, there are problems that *can* be fixed but only *after* we deal with them straight on no matter how painful or upsetting.

My friend Jim Weinraub used to say that "thing" problems were better than "people" problems meaning that situations can be resolved a lot easier than issues involving people. No matter, it is comforting to note that all problems are not created equally and at no time do we have to fix everything that is wrong the moment we discover that it is, indeed, a problem.

From now on all we need to do is line them up as they occur. As unintuitive as it may seem, there is no need to make our problems go away or to resolve them the moment they happen. In fact, as I have said, it may be disadvantageous to do so. It can be liberating and encouraging to realize dealing with life's adversities and working through them is *more* important than wishing them away, being in denial or pressuring yourself to pull a solution out of a hat like a magician produces a rabbit.

2. Use your God-given gifts every minute of every day

There is hardly a person alive who doesn't have at least *one* gift – a special talent, a unique personality or a people skill in some area of life. In fact, most people have many – and I call them gifts not entitlements. A brain surgeon tends to the neurological, a plumber fixes drains, teachers inspire and carpenters build. But our gifts are not just limited to vocations. Compassion, confidence, insight, leadership, patience, humor, ethics and other virtues are often the characteristics that we most admire.

Agnes Gonxha Bojaxhiu was a Catholic nun who founded Missionaries of Charity in India in 1950. Her religious order tended to the poor, the orphaned, the sick and dying. She won the Nobel Peace Prize in 1979 and her good works were eventually taken up by others in over 100 countries where the poor and neglected had no one to turn to other than people who lived every day utilizing the gifts God gave them. This gifted and compassionate person was also known by a more familiar name – Mother Teresa of Calcutta.

It was Mother Teresa who said, *"God doesn't require us to succeed, He only requires that you try."*

It isn't optional to withhold our gifts from society, relationships, workplaces or elsewhere. Gifts are gifts and they are not to be squandered. To me, this concept means everything. It gives purpose to our lives. When we are struggling with questions such as what is the meaning of my life or what do I want to do for a living, the answer becomes apparent.

Use your God-given gifts, the talents and proclivities that make you special without concern for what they may bring you in terms of power, ego or financial reward. It's a simple thought – a mission – that helps add meaning to lives that all too frequently are in need of it even when the person struggling with the issue has been blessed with many gifts.

You might be interested to know that I often reserved the last class of the semester to share with my music industry students at USC this professor's secrets to success. They were very interested. From day one most had Googled Professor Del Colliano and wanted to know all about my career in the media business. They also wanted to hear any advice I might be able to give them as they started their lives on the topic of how to make money and have a successful career.

My answer was simple and to the point: be excellent at something. Be unconcerned with how much money you make or what your title may be. When you try to be excellent at that which you do, good things happen and often you are rewarded in unexpected ways such as financially – yes, that, too!

The second step to a meaningful life, then, is to see it as an obligation not an option to use your God-given gifts, talents and traits every minute of every day.

3. Be grateful for that which you have

"Gratitude unlocks the fullness of life. It turns what we have into enough, and more. It turns denial into acceptance, chaos into order, confusion into clarity... It turns problems into gifts, failures into success, the unexpected into perfect timing and mistakes into important events. Gratitude makes sense of our past, brings peace for today and creates a vision for tomorrow."

– Melody Beattie

The trifecta of a meaningful life is, as Father Martin Padovani calls it, an attitude of gratitude. A spiritual person would say that gratitude is a reminder of God's presence in our lives. That God is always at work on the human condition in His own way. We may doubt His presence but it is nonetheless there at work even when we lose faith.

Gratitude helps us in good times but also in bad times as we remember the good with appreciation. It steadies us at times of great loss or disappointment. There is no time when a good healthy dose of gratefulness is not appropriate. The too-often repeated sentiment that we appreciate things (and people) when we no longer have them has survived the ages because it is true. Gratitude is more important than happiness as incredible as that may seem to some because appreciation is the engine that drives happiness. With gratitude there can be no real happiness. If you doubt it, you can look to the wealthy who have attained their good fortunes by perseverance and dedication to the almighty dollar. Psychiatrists offices are not just filled with the poor and troubled masses. The wealthy and prominent come to find that getting rich was a lot easier than getting happy and happiness is a residue of gratitude.

Gratitude is actually an antidepressant. When you take it or give it, you tend to crowd out negative thoughts. You can't be grateful and unhappy at the same time. That's even better than a pill. And you can never overdose on gratitude.

I am aware that gratitude is a word that has been bandied about in pop culture and in a way may seem trite. Let me separate the overused from the seldom viewed. If you think of gratitude as a gentle prayer of thanks, you are channeling the sincerity that brings positive feelings, self-confidence and even optimism. Gratitude, then, is a thank you expressed many times over and with great sincerity.

When I first met Father Padovani I told him I was not very religious although I described myself as spiritual. In my infinite arrogance I expressed interest only in psychology *without* the religion. But in a magical way and over time, Father Padovani won me to his way of thinking. Do you know how? He ended our many conversations over the years with a prayer of thankfulness. These conversational prayers seemed perfectly comfortable –

after all, he mentioned me in them and the people in my life that I talked about.

What was amazing was how he could also express thanks and concern for people who were troublesome to say the least. One day after a meeting, I wondered was Father Padovani actually praying with me? No. Couldn't be. That was not possible. Or was it? It was then that I came to realize that – call it what you want – gratitude was actually a gentle prayer of thankfulness in good times, bad times, for good people and evil. And that I could not strive for a meaningful life without that attitude for gratitude.

Therefore, I implore you – the third working part to a meaningful life is be grateful for that which you have – even when it isn't much and especially when it isn't much. Gratitude is the final piece to life's difficult puzzle that really only has three pieces as difficult as they are to put together.

To live life to the fullest, deal with your problems, use your God-given gifts and always remember to be grateful for that which you have.

3

GAIN CONTROL BY SUBMISSION

It was Bishop Fulton J. Sheen who said, *"It is one of the paradoxes of creation that we gain control by submission."*

In a world that screams the opposite, it is not surprising that we often miss the wisdom of letting go of things. In a sense, this is a scary thought – a *very* scary thought. The dictionary describes submission as "the action or fact of accepting or yielding to a superior force or to the will or authority of another person." When I first read Bishop Sheen's quote, I thought it was insane. Until, well, until you look around and see how many of us try so hard to have our way. It often makes us miserable and even when we manage to get what we want, we're not always happy.

Nicholas Kristof writing in *The New York Times* in January 2010 declared the happiest people on earth Costa Ricans according to *The World Database of Happiness*. Number one in "happy life years". First in the New Economics Foundation "happy planet index" combining happiness and longevity and adjusted for environmental impact. One might think it is the beautiful beaches of Costa Rica that won the day, but close behind was Denmark – certainly a chillier locale.

Costa Rica puts a premium on education and that may be responsible for the gender equality that is realized in the country. As Kristof observes, *"What sets Costa Rica apart is its remarkable decision in 1949 to dissolve its armed forces and invest instead in education. Increased schooling created a more stable society, less prone to the conflicts that have raged elsewhere in Central America. Education also boosted the economy, enabling the country to become a major exporter of computer chips and improving English-language skills so as to attract American eco-tourists."*

But personal happiness, it would seem, is not being enhanced in countries where their citizens are stressed out and where their lives feel out of control.

Stress leads to health issues, lifestyle concerns and relationship problems. Yet, we are told to work out more, take a Yoga class and chill out. That, *too*, but there is a road not taken on this as well.

Stress is a wake-up call. An opportunity to channel life's frustrations into something very good.

My approach is to give up.

That's right. *Give up control.* Give up having to have our way all the time. Putting a stop to the erroneous notion that being in total control is actually possible. I submit that it is not. And having said that, the secret of a less stressful life is to do the opposite of what we have probably done all of our lives and let go.

Religious people tell us to "Let go and let God". For non-believers, the letting go part still works. It is possible that all along we are creating more stress for ourselves by trying to manage all the things and relationships in our lives that are important to us. I ask, do you really want that job? Full-time?

A friend of mine advising a couple that was so controlling in their personal relationship told them to stop it right now. She said that when you want things to turn out your way – when you want to hear it from the other person the way you have imagined it in *your* mind, then it is tantamount to you writing the script for the dialogue for *both* of you. You are robbed of the love and respect that could come to you, if you would only allow it to be heard of its own free will.

I've been there. On both the right and wrong side of this equation and I can say that the benefits you will receive in submitting to the other person's feelings is greater than the uneasiness you may feel at first.

So how insane is it to practice the art of submission? My goodness, is what I am saying a blow to equality of species? Am I suggesting that we become a world of wimps constantly standing for nothing and always acceding to the will of another?

Not at all.

In fact, it's the other way around. Letting go and becoming more docile to life and to those who disagree with us does not mean we relinquish our strong opinions, values and preferences. Often when you see a couple that is happy – that seems to have it all – you see two opposites thus, the wisdom of opposites attract. But how can opposites attract unless they are spending 24/7 trying to cajole, convince and coerce the other person into being and thinking like them? Ah, therein lies the important difference. It is because the two individuals are opposite and allow each to truly be individuals no matter what they say that is the magic of what makes a good relationship work.

It is more important to be compatible on morals, ethics and values than it is to continuously write the script for others. Therefore, if you are writing the soap opera of your life, wouldn't it be more fun, more exciting, more beneficial to all if you submitted to the feelings, desires and opinions of another so you can enjoy the diversity of your relationship.

I know what you're thinking.

Alright, Jerry, I am with you when it comes to personal relationships but not with professional relationships or friendships. Again, the evidence is there that we lose plenty of sleep over trying to make better friends providing us with fewer disappointments. And we literally spend all of our waking hours trying to make a boss, superior or mentor think of us as valuable and worth paying a large salary to. But it rarely works. Why? *Because it is virtually impossible to write the script for someone else.*

On the other hand, we can manage our words, thoughts and feelings at will.

A traumatic experience I cannot forget was when, as a young on-air broadcasting professional, I was being interviewed for a job in Philadelphia. Everything was going well. The employer asked. I answered. Finally at the end, the prospective employer said, "One of your references doesn't think you're ready for this position." The blood drained out of my body. I turned pale and concerned. Here was my opportunity – with this big prize on the line – to write the script for the reference from hell. Certainly I wouldn't have put his name down as a reference if I had known. Perhaps that has happened to you.

Instead, I gained my composure and in answer to my reference who felt I wasn't ready for the major market broadcasting job I said, "I am very sorry to hear that." Period. Nothing more.

My interviewer said, "Well, he's a jerk anyway. You're hired."

Before you dismiss the value of submitting to reality – whatever it is and whatever is really going on and being said – remember that the number one problem in our world today is the repercussions from stress. From trying to make others think like us, say what we want and do what we want.

You're totally free from this page on if you can stand up and be who you want to be by letting others do the same thing.

Submission to every individuals right to be themselves is like lifting an elephant off your back.

But someday the real nirvana is reached when we can do what Bishop Fulton J. Sheen professes:

"If you will whatever God wills, you will always have exactly what you want. When you want anything else, you are not happy before you get it, and when you do get it, you do not want it. That is why you are up today and down tomorrow."

At the end of the day when you've done everything you can, resignation and acceptance. Trust in God.

4

THE JEALOUSY DIET

"In jealousy there is more self-love than love."
– François VI, Duc de La Rochefoucauld, *Maximes*, 1665

Perhaps the greatest literary work about jealousy was Shakespeare's *Othello*. Circumstantial evidence that can ruin lives. Othello gives in to jealousy when Iago convinces him that Desdemona has been an unfaithful wife. Othello goes on to murder his wife and kill himself. Iago employs jealousy as a motive in riling Othello even though jealousy is probably what prompted Iago's own self-destructive jealousy. Not unlike real life, jealousy is often the problem of the jealous person not the target who attracts jealous feelings. Jealousy is always destructive.

Nothing kills interpersonal relationships more than jealousy.

In extreme cases, people literally kill each other over jealousy. But jealousy also kills the love between two people in a marriage or relationship. There may be little you can do to stave off jealous acts and motives on the part of others, but if you want to be successful and happy, jealousy must be eliminated, reduced or effectively managed.

So what is the difference between jealousy and envy? Jealousy means, "apprehensive or vengeful out of fear of being replaced by someone else." Envy means, "to bear a grudge toward someone due to coveting what that person has or enjoys." Envy. Jealousy. Both of them are bad for you and for relationships.

If we can cutback on carbs or fat in our diets, there must be a way to shed this jealousy. It is dead weight that burdens relationships.

You have no doubt heard the phrase "he or she doesn't have a jealous bone in their body". I'd like to tell you about one that does and one that doesn't.

When legendary television interviewer Barbara Walters became the first woman network TV anchor, a big deal was made out of her million-dollar salary. And while a lot of what happened in that day was gender-related politics, Barbara Walters had to endure on-camera and off the air insults about her pay, gender and speech impediment that would not have been directed at a man. She was obviously qualified for the position but some others including her on-air co-anchor could barely hide their jealousy as Walters was forced to endure public humiliation.

Barbara Walters went on to have a glorious and very prosperous career in television not only as a news personality but also as the creator of a very popular show called *The View*. The same cannot be said of some of her public detractors. I don't know Barbara Walters and I don't know her jealousies, if any, but the inequities that surrounded her career based on other people's psychological problems is a high profile example of what takes place every day in offices, on streets and in cubicles everywhere.

When I worked in local television in Philadelphia, one of the news anchors refused to take a vacation. Let's just say he thought twice before he took time off rather than have anyone else sit in his anchor chair. Was he jealous of others who might have been qualified to take his place or were they jealous of him and waiting for a public audition to get his job?

It wasn't just the high profile business of television where jealousy reared its head. When I was a professor at The University of Southern California, I saw it in academia among professors (tenure track vs. clinical staff, teachers vs. researchers) and even teachers and students. This is not to say that for the most part professors at USC were not focused on being excellent instructors, yet one jealous and arrogant teacher is one too many. It even happens in idyllic settings where ivy grows on the walls.

To be free of this disease is to be truly liberated.

Jealousy is a complicated and involved malady but to the extent that it hurts us from being our best and bringing the best out of others, we need a plan to eliminate or greatly reduce it from our lives, families, relationships and workplaces.

So, if you agree that you want to go on a life long diet to reduce or eliminate jealous tendencies that get in your way, here's how to begin.

Rule 1 – Let go of the fear that you don't have value.

As Jennifer James says, *"Jealousy scans for evidence to prove the point – that others will be preferred and rewarded more than you. There is only one alternative – self-value. If you cannot love yourself, you will not believe that you are loved. You will always think it's a mistake or luck. Take your eyes off others and turn the scanner within. Find the seeds of your jealousy, clear the old voices and experiences. Put all the energy into building your personal and emotional security. Then you will be the one others envy, and you can remember the pain and reach out to them."*

Rule 2 – Repeat often: "Jealousy hurts me more than it hurts them."

William Penn wrote in *Some Fruits of Solitude*, 1693 *"The jealous are troublesome to others, but a torment to themselves."* That is, as destructive as jealousy is to others, it is even more destructive to the jealous person. We are hurting ourselves far more when we exhibit jealousy. Give up jealous tendencies as a matter of self-preservation if nothing else.

Rule 3 – Count jealousies like calories – Make a list of the people of whom you are jealous.

In a food diet, doctors often advise to write down what you eat in a daily log so that the dieter can become aware of which foods are actually causing them to gain weight. So it is with the Jealousy Diet. Make a list that you do not have to share with anyone that contains the names of people of whom you suspect you may be jealous of. Look to work, friendships, personal relationships and family.

Look at the list every day and grade the level of jealousy on a scale of 1 to 10 – 10 being so bad that the target of your jealousy must take leave of you. Then, on a daily basis review your list and cross out a number when you can revise it up or down – say, when a 5 becomes a 4. Becoming conscious of your behavior and grading yourself often will provide the most important stimulus to making a change. Quite often jealousy is subconscious making it very hard to deal with. Counting jealousies like calories helps with that.

Rule 4 – Focus on your accomplishments.

"Envy is the art of counting the other fellow's blessings instead of your own" (Harold Coffin). The Jealousy Diet is about counting your own blessings – so much the better to make you less likely to display the envy that rises above the surface like an iceberg in the North Atlantic. An iceberg, after all, is predominantly below the surface of the ocean – that means as massive as most icebergs are to the eye, it is what cannot be seen below the surface that is even more destructive should an ocean liner run into it.

Every calendar or mobile application makes it easy to document the many things we accomplish every day. But it is usually our failures that we remember and we don't need to write them down because we often let them haunt us over and over again. It's easy to change the focus by keeping track of the big and little things that we accomplish daily. It serves as a disincentive to be needy and jealous giving us the best results from The Jealousy Diet.

Rule 5 – Make amends for jealous behavior.

When you lapse, as we all do, look for ways to make it right again. Making amends is actually more important to you than to the target of your jealousies. Bet you'll feel a bit better, too.

I reiterate – *jealousy kills.*

Careers. Relationships. Self-confidence.

Our success is not assured by someone else's failure.

Go on a life long Jealousy Diet and relieve yourself of the dead weight that kills relationships.

5

THE SHAME GAME

If jealousy kills relationships, shame kills self-esteem.

You've no doubt heard the exclamation – "shame on you", perhaps by a parent or a friend. And, actually, when someone else is shaming you, as bad as it sounds, it is not as destructive as what happens when we shame ourselves.

Marilyn J. Sorensen, Ph.D and author of *Breaking the Chain of Low Self-Esteem* says, *"Individuals with low self-esteem become overly sensitive and fearful in many situations…They are afraid they won't know the rules or that they've blundered, misspoken or acted in ways others might consider inappropriate. Or they might perceive that others reject or are critical of them."* Dr.

Sorensen says that once low self-esteem is inflicted on a child, they experience "self-esteem attacks" in the form of embarrassment or shame.

"Unlike guilt – which is the feeling of doing something wrong," according to Dr. Sorensen, *"shame is the feeling of being something wrong."*

We often misunderstand the difference between guilt and shame.

Guilt occurs when we feel badly about our actions often prompting us to take some form of remedial action. In other words, guilt is not as detrimental to the human condition as is shame and may even be helpful.

Shame makes us feel badly about ourselves often leaving us humiliated. Shame can feed damaging co-dependent relationships with ourselves and others giving other people permission to act in an abusive way.

All of us experience or have experienced shame directed at us. Then we repeat the insult of shame over and over in our subconscious to our own disadvantage.

I heard a young speaker tell her audience that she grew up in a household where her father took all the doors off their hinges – even the bathrooms. One might think that because the entire family grew up under these bizarre circumstances that she would be "shameless". Not so. As she told it, the opposite occurred. She carried around an overwhelming sense of shame for the functions that others would describe as natural – a burden she never asked for.

That's one of the reasons why overcoming the urge to shame ourselves and stopping others from trying to do it is so important. You don't have to have the doors taken off to become unhinged. Shame is a killer of our spirit and makes us a slave to comments from others that eventually can control our self-esteem.

And no matter who we are, no person is immune.

In school, isn't it amazing how the class bully finds exactly the right insult to shame his or her unwitting victims? I had crooked teeth as I was growing up and you guessed it, the class bully in seventh grade zeroed in on my teeth like a laser beam. Today my teeth are straight and white yet I can still feel the pain of being told I was ugly. And believe me, bullies don't use human relations principles when they are pushing you around.

There are opportunities for people to play the shame game all around us.

Married, then divorced? I've heard more than one ex say to their partners, "I feel sorry for the next person who marries you." That makes no sense. Divorce is about two people not having the love, maturity and skill to be with each other. It surely doesn't mean that there isn't another person with whom you are compatible. Shamed in divorce, the survivor goes on to future relationships with baggage that even U.S. Airways wouldn't check. Shame like this is not based on fact. It is meant to hurt and cripple or damage the victim going on.

I use the term victim because people who are the target of shamemeisters also become victims of their *own* self-destruction.

The shame many unemployed people feel when they lose their livelihood and careers is widespread and growing. Recently, my daughter was commuting from New York City to Philadelphia and within a six-week period of time, two people in separate incidents threw themselves in front of a speeding Amtrak train in the northeast corridor. It is hard to know the exact reasons for their despair but careers that end with the humiliation that comes from the loss of employment can cause acts of desperation.

More commonly, the depressing visit to the unemployment line and feelings that surround not being able to pull your weight or deal with others who are still employed result in silent suffering. Therefore, human beings can be shamed by an impersonal act such as a company downsizing in a recession simply by the act of being let go – even if it had little to do with their value as an employee instead of the employer in financial trouble.

Not being a good parent has shame written all over it and you hear that a lot today, but what exactly is a good parent? Can a divorced father or mother or single working parent be a good parent? Of course. But from the mouth of a person using this challenging opportunity as a moment to shame you, it is an unwarranted way to beat a person down who is actually trying to step it up.

The fascinating thing about shame is that once we've been a victim of it, we can heap tons of shame upon ourselves and unfortunately on others.

There is no place in our lives for shame. Not a single redeeming thing. Nothing to be gained. Self-esteem ready to be diminished.

Sydney Smith, author of *Lecture on the Evil Affections* reminds us, *"The most curious offspring of shame is shyness."* Perhaps that's why the term, "secretive, silent and shameful" has entered our lexicon. Shame takes many prisoners.

There are four effective ways to deal with shame.

1. Accept your faults only as long as you can name an equal number of good virtues. Concentrating on faults alone leaves you vulnerable to shame. *"Everyone has his faults which he continually repeats, neither fear nor shame can cure them",* says the French poet Jean de La Fontaine. The best plan is to always give thanks for the good things about you while you vow to work on the faults that we all have in the human condition. This is a way to balance the ledger and make it more difficult to fall victim to people or circumstances that promote the shame that hurts our lives.

2. Avoid becoming co-dependent to another person. The quick and easy way to do this is to take charge of how you feel about *you* as a person. Codependent people earn their name because they rely on others to validate that they are good. If you need your partner to say you are beautiful, hot or good looking, then you've given that person a lot of power they don't need. Instead, believe in your own virtues – in this case your appearance – and when someone else compliments you, they are simply seconding what you *already* know. That is healthy. And healthy people have a built-in armor against shame.

3. No one – like in no one – gets your permission to act in an abusive way. Physical and psychological abuse are too often tolerated and accepted by the victim which enables the shame that results. The moment you sense someone is out of order, they are out of order. Stop the discussion. Stop the abuse. Stop the relationship. No good can come from abusive people and abuse stops when you say "no more". When I worked in television and radio news in Philadelphia, we used to monitor the police radio for crime stories. Often a call would be sent out to squad cars being dispatched to domestic disputes. Sometimes, we were told, officers would arrive in the middle of a heated argument where words were exchanged or bodily harm inflicted. Police officers hated these calls more than any others. They walked in, broke up the warring partners and, frequently once the partner was saved from their abuser, the victim would side with the abuser and turn on the police officers. Therefore, as incredible as it

may seem, victims often promulgate the abuse and enable their abusers.

4. Love of self is the antidote for shame. The more you cultivate and appreciate the fine person you are – faults and all – the less likely you will be a victim of living with the debilitating residue of shame.

Shame kills self-esteem. Love of self kills shame.

6

THE HAPPINESS FORMULA

You take a lot of courses in college but after you graduate often very few remain memorable.

You may remember some of the teachers – positively or negatively.

But the subject matter? Well, that's another story.

No doubt you have a few courses you remember from your education and I have one I'd like to share.

I was fortunate to elect a course at Temple University called General Semantics with Professor Harry Weinberg.

Professor Weinberg as I remember him had a speech impediment – perhaps from a stroke – that required him to speak very deliberately and for his students to listen with a keen ear. Weinberg was also an author of a textbook called *Levels of Knowing and Existence* and while the title may put you off, the book is so good I still have it and re-read it regularly.

Life has a way of dashing our hopes. Of leaving us disappointed even after we've given everything we have to achieve our goals. Perhaps that means a good job and money to live. But even hard workers wind up on the unemployment line every now and then. Or maybe we dream of a wonderful relationship, a family but somehow it eludes us. Partners cheat. Individuals grow apart. Children are often the unwitting victims. All of this and our intentions were good.

It follows that when life hands you a lemon, sometimes you don't want to make lemonade. You just want to throw your hands up in the air and say, "What more do I have to do?" or "What did I do wrong?"

This leads to discouragement that can wreck even the best-intentioned person.

Weinberg's gift to me and his students was to prove to us the importance of keeping our motivation high while keeping our expectations in check – no matter what we pursued in life. Weinberg argued that if we did, we would avoid the real highs and real lows and as a result be happier.

That is, often our unfulfilled dreams were not the cause of our unhappiness but rather the let down that comes when we aim high and expect the reward to follow.

A friend of mine who also took the course became proficient at keeping his expectations down – so good at it that he spent a lifetime without much joy. That's counterproductive, too.

My take on Weinberg's message was to pursue that which I wanted to accomplish, but never assume that the results would be assured. Often, people think if they work hard then it follows that they will get what they want. When they don't, they become depressed and worse yet – demotivated.

Competitors playing sports don't show up at the stadium or arena and say, "If I play hard, we win." Even if they do, that is a guarantee that cannot be made – just as in life. Instead, a more workable solution is to show up, play hard and *hope* to win. After all, there is always another day.

That's it!

I took Weinberg's course so I now know the secret to full achievement and happiness, right?

I loved this course so much I just knew I would do well in it. And Weinberg broke the grading into two components as memory serves me. A grade for the final paper and a grade for applying the principle he taught.

Well, it sounded like an "A" to me.

Unfortunately, not to Professor Weinberg who gave me a good grade on one component and a lousy one on the other.

Ah ha! My first test of keeping expectations low and motivation high.

In life we seem to either expect doom and gloom or in the alternative that which we want. My observation has been that neither is true and setting our life's compass to these extremes is extremely hazardous to our success and happiness.

So what's wrong with a few unfulfilled dreams now and again? The more elusive they are, the more we learn about ourselves and when we eventually prevail, we do so with a far greater appreciation. Therefore, the best approach to success and happiness is to work hard without consideration to what you may accomplish.

Keeping your expectations low and motivation high also eliminates the need for luck. "Luck, as Branch Rickey, the Major League Baseball executive said, is the residue of design" – that is, we make our own good luck.

And I believe good luck happens through hard work.

So, if you want to always be ready to play your "A" game, don't count the winning score until the end of the contest.

To help smooth out life's highs and lows for the benefit of your own mental well being:

1. Train yourself to focus on the goal without assuming the result. It's fine to see vividly in your mind's eye that which you want to accomplish, just don't tie your effort on any one day to the "expected" result.

2. Practice on something minor – don't just jump in and see if Weinberg's advice works for you on the day your presentation is due at work. Or, for that matter, maybe that is a good time for you to give up control of the end result and replace it with a well-played "game".

3. Think of five situations in which you wound up being disappointed after giving your best effort. Recall what it felt like to work so hard and expect the end result to be everything you anticipated. Once you bring these feelings back alive, you may agree that it is best to control that which you can (your effort) rather than assuming the result that is often out of your total control.

4. List five circumstances under which you could benefit from keeping your expectations low and motivation high. A love relationship, perhaps? The quest for a new job? Your desire to be a great parent? That promotion? Believe me, the hard part about this assignment is coming up with only five ways.

**Dream on, but keep your motivation high
and your expectations low.**

7

MAKING YOUR OWN GOOD LUCK

Did you ever hear someone say, "If I didn't have bad luck, I'd have no luck at all"?

Now, there is emerging evidence from the University of Cologne that belief in a superstition may in some cases improve results of activities over which individuals have some control.

That is, you can wear that retro team jersey to the World Series but the fact that it is you wearing it and not the batter in the bottom of the ninth inning with two runners on and two outs will likely have no effect on the outcome of the game.

In one intriguing example, University of Cologne researchers handed a "lucky" golf ball to participants as part of a study only to find that the "lucky" golfers sank two more putts on the average than a control group – a 35% performance improvement just from thinking their golf ball was lucky!

Lucky bracelets and charms are growing in popularity and one wonders if these new aids actually work. In the same study, 30% of those playing a test memory game did far better than those who did not and even more interesting is that they felt 30% more capable than those who played without the benefit of lucky charms.

This must be the answer, then – wear lucky charms, give in to superstitions and you'll find the key to succeeding in life.

However – and I'll bet you saw this coming – it's not as simple as that.

Sure, Tiger Woods can wear a red shirt for good luck on the last day of each tournament but if you or I wore that shirt in the same event the result would be far different. After all, Woods may be down on his luck on personal matters, but even a red shirt doesn't allow him to win *every* Sunday unless he believes it. Or his sponsor Nike does.

What is significant is that whenever people *believe* that they can do better, they apparently *can* do better.

The mind is a terrible thing to fill with negative thoughts.

Look no further than the simple sugar pill – the ultimate medical mirage that defies imagination. When medical drug trials are conducted, it is customary for one group of people to be given the real drug and a separate group the placebo. Neither group knows whether they are getting the actual medicine or a sugar pill, as laypeople like to call it.

In the January 6, 2010, weekly edition of *The Journal of the American Medical Association* in which an analysis was presented for six clinical trials of antidepressants from 1980 through 2009, the conclusion was that people with mild or moderate depression improved when they took their medicine. But the improvement was identical whether they were taking the actual drug or a placebo that looked just like the medicine. In cases where testers had more severe symptoms, the real drug did slightly better than the placebo. There were 718 patients in the study according to an account in *Consumer Reports* (July 2010).

The power of suggestion is obviously a potent remedy in and of itself. You can take two aspirins and call me in the morning, thank you!

Dale Carnegie knew that you give a person a reputation to live up to instead of one to live down. This mental adjustment changes the dynamics of interpersonal relationships.

Coaches can inspire their players by conveying a belief in themselves as winners. The world of sports supplies many examples. As a hockey fan, I am always aware of the message Flyers Head Coach Fred Shero posted on the wall in the locker room before they played to win the Stanley Cup in the 70's – *"Win together today and we walk together forever."* About 35 years later, the same Philadelphia Flyers became only the third team in National Hockey League history to win a seven game series after the opposing team – in this case the Boston Bruins – took a commanding 3-0 lead. Imagine the positive attitudes it must have taken to come back from the brink of elimination game after game.

Norman Vincent Peale wrote the best-selling book *The Power of Positive Thinking* and it was Napoleon Hill that said, *"Whatever the mind can conceive and believe, it can achieve."*

So what's luck got to do with it?

Apparently when we *believe* we are going to be lucky, then we are *luckier.*

I wish I could say it worked for gambling and casino games but even though some players think it works sometimes, the house *always* comes out the winner.

Now, as we've learned, there is clinical proof. But you don't really need research to tell you that when you believe in something positive good things happen and conversely when you don't, the self fulfilling prophecy rears its ugly head.

So out with bad luck and in with good luck. Thinking makes it so or at the very least seems to help. If we adjust the way we think, we expect to do better. Instead of fearing the bad things that often happen in life, marshal the forces of good luck that we have within our power to channel.

Maybe we've got luck all wrong anyway. Ever notice that people with the nickname "Lucky" are not really lucky at all? "Lucky" Luciano, born Salvatore Lucania, was a mobster and first official boss of the Genovese mafia family in New York City. What was so lucky about this early 20th century don? He ran a crime syndicate but also spent time in jail, fled the country, had personal tragedy when his girlfriend died of breast cancer and *he* dropped dead at Naples Airport of a heart attack.

Luciano notoriously earned his nickname when in 1929 he was forced into a limo at gunpoint, beaten and stabbed and dumped on a beach on New York Bay. Luciano survived the murder attempt earning him the name "Lucky". I think I would rather be unlucky if I had to earn the nickname the way "Lucky" Luciano did.

Branch Rickey had it right when he said, *"Luck is the residue of design"* meaning we make our own good luck. As contrary as that sounds to the popular notion of being unexpectedly struck by good fortune, Rickey is suggesting that days, weeks, months and years of preparation is that which paves the way for good things to happen. And the more luck we are brewing at any given time, the more good things are likely to emerge over time. This belief is the opposite of standing around and hoping for dumb luck that happens unintentionally or without planning.

That makes smart luck the stuff of hard work, positive mental attitudes, rejection of negative thoughts and faith that no matter how bad things actually get, we have the power in between our ears to make them better now. *This minute.* And with it comes an immediate benefit – increased confidence that somehow, someway we know there is a reward coming if we will persevere and endure.

Confidence is that perishable quality that seems like you'll never lose it when you've got it and when you lose it, it sometimes seems like you'll never get it back.

From now on, channel your good luck even if you have to be superstitious. Betting against yourself reduces the odds of success.

Remarkably enough, simply thinking and believing that you have an edge, gives you the edge.

8

REMEMBER THE TED WILLIAMS PRINCIPLE

"Baseball is the only field of endeavor where a man can succeed three times out of ten and be considered a good performer." – Ted Williams

I think the old proverb *"Nothing succeeds like success"* is a problem.

I mean, it sounds great as a proverb and, by the way, aren't all proverbs *old*?

That's one of the things messing with our minds these days, that everyone is a success. Failure is not an option.

Not so.

Wynn Etter, my longtime friend and Dale Carnegie sponsor in Cherry Hill, New Jersey used to hand out a business card with the Henry David Thoreau quote, *"None are so old as those who have outlived enthusiasm."*

Today the next generation is taught that everything they do is right. There are no losers, only winners and self-esteem is built through constant positive reinforcement of validating thoughts whether merited or not.

I offer a different view of success, failure and self-esteem.

Losing can be a character builder. Adversity introduces a person to him or herself and to those around them. Winning the soccer match is wonderful. Losing it can be a motivator for next time. But, as has happened in the last decade, when children are raised in scholastic sports competitions without a winner or loser, then there are no benefits to take with you in life.

The sentiment on the part of parents and others to buck up their children's self-esteem by avoiding failure is a noble thought – just not very effective.

Failure is the best rehearsal for success.

I didn't say it was fun.

The only time failure is permanent is when we give up and stop trying. Therefore, looked at in this light, perhaps you can see how important failing at something can be to a successful person.

On the other hand, imagine going through life without the safety net of hearing you're always right, smart, good looking and athletic. The moment we run into reality, our real success is knocked off course.

My mother, a little old Italian woman, never rescued me from anything. I would have liked being saved from myself more often, but it wasn't in her DNA. She sent me to the school of hard knocks because she knew it taught lessons and built character. Not that mom couldn't have lightened up a little bit, but even if she could read this book today that was not a possibility. Yet in her old world approach she really felt that getting up off the floor and standing up to fight another day was a virtue. I look back on whatever success I might have had so far in life and owe it to my mom for that.

Once a friend of mine, known as Butch, sucker punched me good and plenty in the neighborhood where I grew up. I ran home crying to my mom hopelessly out of breath from the beating.

A few hugs would have been nice, but no – she wasn't in the mood for that. Instead, mom sent me back out immediately to stand up to the bully. Not knowing what to do, I obediently directed myself to the backyard where I walked up to Butch and punched this big bully right in *his* stomach. I was a skinny kid and no threat for sure, but Butch fell down to the ground. I learned from that moment on that bullies always backed off when you stood up to them.

Failure is not always about money or career. Often it is about the self-doubts that plague us in life.

I used to remind my students at USC who came to their professor for personal advice that they were talking to a man who had been married *three* times. I asked them, "Are you sure you want advice from this man?" Always I heard something like, "Well, you certainly know what *not* to do in matters of love." I retorted, "You're just desperate, go on …" and they laughed.

Fail at one marriage and fail at the next and if you don't give up and try hard to be better, you then find that a happy marriage – the one I eventually found – is not a pipe dream but an expectation.

Get fired from your job – as many of my friends in the entertainment industry have experienced in their careers – and you feel as if there is something wrong with *you*. It is your fault. You blew it. In fact, you may or may not have led to your own career demise but it isn't the end of the world. *Remember, failure isn't permanent until you stop trying.*

One of the things I always remember whenever things go wrong works 100% of the time. I'd like to share it with you.

Ted Williams was one of the best hitters in baseball. One year he batted .406. That is remarkable for baseball – getting on base 40% of the time.

And that's what does it for me.

The best hitter in one epic season succeeded *only* 40% of the time and he was one of the greatest to play the game. Looked at another way, the great Ted Williams *failed* 60% of the time when he was at his very best.

I also like to remind myself that in baseball today, ballplayers are compensated to the tune of millions of dollars when they hit for batting averages of .250 – or succeed at getting on base just 25% of the time. Are they multi-million dollar failures or are they successes who tolerate strike outs, fly outs and foul outs to play another day succeeding a mere one-fourth of the time?

So, if the best ever succeeded just 40% of the time in his greatest baseball season and players are called a success when they succeed 25% of the time or *less,* then I thought maybe I should revisit what success really is.

Does this work for you the way it does for me?

Additionally, sometimes a player only needs to hit a homerun to win the important game, but he or she may only be a .200 hitter every other time they come to bat. Therefore, there is a virtue in coming through in the clutch when you're needed – even if you haven't done so consistently before.

Our view of success tends to guarantee failure.

We will do just about anything to *avoid* failing even if it means not trying or taking the safe road. Of course, we should always want to succeed. I do. You do. But the gift that keeps on giving is the one you give yourself when you recognize and live by your new motto: *"Failure isn't permanent until you stop trying."*

Sometimes in my social life I would be devastated when someone I was interested in rejected or avoided me. What could it be? Was I not handsome enough? Athletic enough? Smart enough? What did I *not* have enough of?

On the other hand when I was on a hot streak – as sometimes happens in relationships – it was funny how much confidence I had because someone *else* thought I was acceptable.

That was wrong then even though I didn't realize it.

But now I know that what someone else thinks of us is far less important than what we think of ourselves. If I hadn't believed that I would be a good husband to a good woman then God only knows how my life would have been so much less rich for me. *I* had to believe it first. And by believe it I am not talking about a pep talk but a deep-seated belief that I was a unique individual simply waiting to meet another one who appreciated me.

Yet I've seen people young and old devastated by divorce and shipwrecked by self-doubt because someone else had a problem with the best they had to offer. After going through two divorces I know that good people may not always be good for each other. Finding the right one requires a little self-love first.

One of the biggest relationship wreckers is being codependent to another person. Codependency has been written about for years as the culprit it is in relationships. However, codependency is less likely to occur in people who do not rely on others to supply them with the traits they think they do not have.

That's why a guy can tell a gal, "You are the most beautiful person in the world" after their first few meetings and then marry that girl and say, "Your abs need a little a work, don't you think?" A healthy person would say, "You look after your abs, I'll look after mine". But all too frequently in the codependent, they were attracted to the "most beautiful person line" because they may not have believed it in the first place.

Off to the gym they go to work on their abs.

That's why it is not uncommon to see that beauty queens, actresses and models often have low self-esteem.

What kind of a world makes that possible? One where we have the inability to accept our own looks – whatever they are.

I used to marvel at beauty contests where the first runner up and the rest of the finalists were apparently chopped liver compared to the winner. Our eyes tell us that isn't so. What, then is beauty? What is intelligence? What is personality?

Was the 50th entrant in the Miss USA pageant the ugliest? Absurd! As the Temptations' song goes, "beauty's only skin deep – yeah, yeah, yeah".

So in our next iteration wouldn't it be wonderful to work as hard on accepting that which we are while working on that which we want to be? Not what someone else wants us to be? *Not* what well-meaning friends and loved ones think we should be just because they love us.

The secret is – look forward more to your next time at bat than whether you are going to hit a home run.

In life, we have successes and failures. Our averages go up and down over time.

To change the way you look at failure starting now, consider the following:

Think of the greatest athlete in any sport and recognize the number of times they fail before they achieve what they want. Then make that strategy yours. Remember the great baseball player Ted Williams in his best effort ever failed 60% of the time.

Build a reminder system into your daily life so you are constantly reminded that times at bat (chances to do things) are more important than hitting home runs (getting what you want when you want it).

Starting right now, begin to accept that your beauty, looks, brains, talent, personality, compassion and other traits are plenty good and of interest to people who will then appreciate you.

When failure hurts (and there is value in feeling some of that pain, believe it or not), consider adopting the attitude, "My victory will eventually be sweeter when I succeed in the future."

Unfair, poorly timed and particularly harsh breaks in life are potential knockout punches to our ego and our success. Life is not fair – plain and simple. Allow yourself time to heal from life's hurts and use whatever spirituality you can muster to remind yourself that a Higher Power can help you through the tough times.

From this moment on, never allow anyone to make you codependent to them (or make someone else codependent to you). Codependency kills relationships and smothers happiness. Whenever anyone accepts you at first and then puts you down subsequently put an end to that line of conversation right then and there. If a person close to you continues to build you up buttercup just to let you down, get rid of them as a friend. When you can't terminate the abusive relationship, put distance between you and the abuser. Sometimes we can't divorce our family or our boss but we can put nine degrees of separation between us. And in the case of the boss, we can ask for a transfer or find a new job if necessary.

Keep in mind that every opportunity to fail is a rehearsal for your eventual success.

You've no doubt heard all the inspirational stories online and visualized on YouTube about "failures" that eventually became successes. Abe Lincoln comes to mind because he failed at just about everything he did in his career and personal life and kept coming back for more. They had few psychiatrists in Lincoln's day. Whatever Honest Abe had, he had plenty of it. Gumption? Maybe. But after literally failing at everything he did Abraham Lincoln was elected president of the United States.

How fortunate for our country.

Lincoln must have believed that he was destined for something good if he kept on trying.

His success was short lived because Lincoln, one of America's greatest and most pivotal presidents, was assassinated while serving his term.

Tragic as that is, it is also significant.

If all we hope for whether in relationships, career or life is one overriding goal; we may ultimately achieve it and find that the benefits of the success we craved are short lived.

Therefore, if we can value the time we have on this earth and learn to enjoy playing the game of life more than having to win every time, we have redefined the meaning of success.

And isn't that what we want to do – reinvent ourselves to be happier and more successful with most of the gifts we already possess.

**The only average that counts
is batting a 1.000 at trying.**

9

THAT RECORDER STICKING OUT OF YOUR HEAD

When I was the program director at a Philadelphia radio station, I will never forget a gentleman – a neighbor, actually, who lived near our transmitter and radio towers. He angrily walked into the station one day to complain.

No, not about the music we were broadcasting.

It seems this listener was a program director's dream – he claimed he couldn't turn the music *off* in his head.

How great was that?

For *me*, that is.

For him, it drove him nuts. Never mind that the station's format was Top 40 and played the same hits over and over again.

You see, this poor soul had a war injury that caused him to need a plate inserted in his head and somehow, some way, the proximity of his "new head" to our powerful 50,000 watt transmitter, was driving him to distraction.

I thought it was a joke at first, but came to look at his predicament differently. Obviously, I couldn't shut the station down or move it and he wasn't about to sell his home nearby so all I could do was play the right records – over and over again.

Strange imagery that got me to thinking.

In many ways we all carry a recorder or a chip around in our heads.

We can't see it, but it's there.

I can prove it because when a young student comes home from school and tells his or her parents, "I got three A's and one B", guess what the *very* next question almost always is?

Not, "Tell me about your A's."

Sadly, it's "What did you get a B in?"

See, I know we have recording devices in our heads because then these youngsters play it over and over again – "What did you get the B in?" Maybe they embellish it the next morning when they wake up, "I'm not a good enough student for my parents."

Of course, this isn't an isolated incident at just one point in our life. The chip repeats itself in a continuous loop and to make matters worse, we never run out of storage capacity for things other people say about us. But we should.

Like when our boss says, "You didn't make your quota last month." That seems to get recorded directly onto the invisible microchip in our brain. Forget that we made our quotas for the past 24 months. But the one we play back and unfortunately remember is "You didn't make your quota *last* month."

And that's another odd thing – why is it that we readily let almost anyone record messages directly into our psyche and we don't?

I had a friend paint a vivid word picture that is most memorable and I'd like to share it with you now in the hope that you won't be able to get this picture out of your mind, either.

My forehead with a big tape, CD or digital mobile device sticking half way out of my skin.

That's the picture we want to conjure up the next time we turn over the right to whisper hurtful or self-limiting things directly in our head. I'm not saying *never* record a negative thought – especially if it is something that you would like to work on and improve. Just don't let anyone else do it.

From now on – what gets into your head is in your possession. You own and control that valuable recording device. Your mind is an asset not a liability created by thoughtless or unhelpful comments from others. From this moment on – *you* are the master of your own tape, CD or recording device that you now know is the one sticking out of your forehead at least in your mind's eye.

Many dysfunctional relationships begin when an individual gives up control of that personal recording mechanism.

The young man who constantly tells his true love that she is the nicest person he has ever met. There is nothing wrong with the sentiment, but codependency creeps in when familiarity causes this party to be emboldened and change his story and tells her she's maybe not always so nice – maybe even mean or hurtful.

Hey, cupid changed his tune and he's doing it right in your brain.

So the increasingly codependent person lives for the approval she once got and potentially loses self-esteem, happiness and possibly even whatever love she thought she had when they first met.

When you record your *own* messages, and someone tells you, "You're the nicest person I have ever met", you decide to say it into the recording device known as your mind – "I have met a person who thinks I am very nice – she's so observant."

In other words, any compliment now becomes a substantiation of what you *already* think of yourself and who you are. No longer do you have to rely on someone else who may be up one day and down the next. No more being codependent to another person.

I've heard the words – maybe you have, too – "I feel sorry for the person who marries you". Sound familiar?

Let's see how you're doing with Recording Messages 101.

What would you say? What would you do?

How about erasing that recording the moment someone uttered those words at you. Hit erase. Then rerecord, "The person I marry gets a great mate – if I decide to marry."

We're using examples of how letting the wrong people record detrimental messages in our minds relating to personal and social issues can be devastating, but believe me, it happens a lot in our careers as well.

I know of a disc jockey who – as the tale goes – worked in Waco, TX and often when he got off the air, one of the stations advertising salesmen would come up to him and criticize his show. As a radio and television performer I can tell you that thin skins are not an asset in a profession where everyone can hear what you do for living. This d.j. finally had enough of it and hauled off and punched the criticizer in the face. For which, legend has it, he wound up paying for his facial reconstruction.

There's a better and cheaper way to put a stop to irritating and critical people who get under our skin and it doesn't involve a left hook. No reason to get stomachaches or high blood pressure over ignorant comments on the job.

That's why one of the best lessons is to learn to appreciate how sensitive and vulnerable we are to hurtful, jealous, unhelpful and mean comments that eventually erode our spirit and self-esteem. Once you see the picture image of that recording device in your head you will wrestle back control of it.

In the future, compliments will be meaningful because they will validate what you already know about your fine self. And criticism can even be more productive if you are the one to acknowledge in advance that something needs improving. Dale Carnegie always said, *"Don't criticize, condemn or complain"* and he's the master of human relations. If Dale Carnegie knows criticism will do no good, then why don't we adopt a new rule that says even constructive criticism is not worth it?

The only time a fault is worth pointing out is if *you* point it out to yourself – and record it as something you want to work on.

The mind is mightier than any other tool we have in life.

Why rent it out to interlopers – many of whom do not have our best interests at heart.

Take control of what is said about you by limiting access of what others are allowed to say directly into your head. Erase hurtful and unhelpful comments. From now on, only you get to record messages directly into your mind.

If we reinvent the way we talk to ourselves, others will take their rightful places in our lives and we will constantly feel good about who we are.

Back in the 80's, President Ronald Reagan's Secretary of State, Alexander Haig, rushed to the White House after an assassin tried to shoot and kill the president. It was a moment of great turmoil and Haig was later criticized for trying to reassure the American people on television by standing before the cameras and saying, *"I'm in charge here."* It looked like a power grab to some, but others felt he was just trying to reassure a terrified nation.

Be Alexander Haig.

When it comes to what gets into your psyche, be in charge.

10

CAREER CHAOS

"The best careers advice to give to the young is 'Find out what you like doing best and get someone to pay you for doing it.'" – Katherine Whitehorn

Thomas Edison, the inventor of the light bulb, was called "Too stupid to learn anything" by teachers during his early education. Edison lived up to his low expectations by being fired from his first two jobs – some say for not being productive. It took Edison over 1,000 failures to complete the experiment that gave us the light bulb.

Albert Einstein and Charles Darwin were also considered failures. Einstein didn't speak until he was four or read until he was seven. You may know the rest of the story. Einstein won the Nobel Prize and revamped the world of physics. Darwin was criticized by none other than his own father for being lazy. Darwin later wrote, *"I was considered by all my masters and my father, a very ordinary boy, rather below the common standard of intellect."* Darwin is known for his scientific studies that concluded that over the ages all species of life descended from common ancestors. Pretty advanced thinking for an "ordinary" boy.

Unfortunately, there is no shortage of examples of people who for one reason or the other should not have achieved what they eventually went on to achieve.

Bud Bilanich a career coach, tells how J.K. Rowling, author of the *Harry Potter* novels was *"Penniless, severely depressed, divorced, trying to raise a child on her own while attending school and writing a novel."* Perhaps all that stress and duress was exactly what it took for Rowling to become a prolific writer who went from welfare to become one of the richest writers in the world in a period of only five years.

Career chaos can start early in life when those close to us or who are most influential such as teachers make an incorrect assessment of human potential. Often – *too often* – the target of these faulty judgments have their lives negatively impacted. In other cases, determination and grit turn perceived disadvantages into advantages, our common theme in this book.

Microsoft founder and billionaire Bill Gates dropped out of Harvard. Apple co-founder and CEO Steve Jobs dropped out of Reed College after one semester on his way to a career that made him billions.

But roadblocks to success do not only plague the rich and famous. They affect everyone. Women have had their careers sidetracked because of a double standard in the business world and because they have frequently held two simultaneous careers – their job *and* raising children. Today, the gender gap is closing. Men are taking more of a role in child-rearing and companies are slowly becoming more cognizant of the importance of leveling the playing field.

Careers go up and down like roller coasters but all it takes is one striking blow and the course of your life can be altered forever whether it is at the beginning, middle or end. In the radio industry, thousands of talented professionals were fired during media consolidation. Radio stations began piping in programming from other cities to save salaries and owners became proficient at using technology to do voice tracking, the science of having an air personality record intros and outros of music from one location for many different cities virtually fooling the audience that thinks what they are hearing is actually local. One air personality can do voice tracking for many radio stations every day for pennies on the dollar. It's hard to have a sustaining career when pay declines and jobs are hard to find.

I have heard that recessions and economic downturns occur roughly every ten years. Obviously, they are not all the 1929 Great Depression, but these economic slumps uproot families, shortchange their children of an education and many times require job retraining to find gainful employment during the ensuing recovery.

My father had only three jobs in his life and one included a 20-year stint in the military serving overseas for four consecutive years. I had that many jobs by the time I was 25. Today, Generation Y, which was heavily hit by the recession, is able and willing but jobs are not available. At one point in 2010 it was estimated that over 30% of that young generation could not find employment.

So whether it's a career interrupted by firing, child rearing or underemployment, career chaos can be disastrous to the human spirit. When I went to Temple University in Philadelphia Professor Lew Klein surprised freshmen and graduates when he told us that before our broadcasting careers were over we would be fired at least five times. We may have considered the comment a joke at the time, but Professor Klein was not kidding. As Executive Producer of Dick Clark's *American Bandstand*, he knew the ups and downs of television.

In the previous age of gold watches at retirement parties where employees were celebrated for their loyalty and devotion to the company, today's worker has discovered that blindly being loyal to a corporation that doesn't return the feeling is bad strategy.

The father of modern management, Peter Drucker, writing in his 1954 book *The Practice of Management* said, *"A man should never be appointed into a managerial position if his vision focuses on people's weaknesses rather than on their strengths."* I'll take that one step further. A person should never seek a position if his or her vision focuses on their *own* weaknesses rather than strengths.

In my work with young people at The University of Southern California, one of the most anticipated classes was the final session. I know what you're thinking. Well, not just for the obvious reason but because I promised to share my view of how to get ahead in life and in their careers. Over time I discovered that my students were succeeding more often than not because they were taking a different approach to their careers.

Here's what I told them:

Rule #1 – Become a Free Agent.

Sports stars do it. Because of Curt Flood and his challenge to Major League Baseball that ultimately led to today's free agent system, you, too, can become a free agent in your line of work off the field. Juxtaposition what your fathers and grandfathers used to do – work for a handful of companies in their lifetime – with parceling out your talents, services and work ethic one year at a time. I do this. My students began to do it, too. Here's how.

Create the four seasons of your business life (by the way, this works well with life in general as you will see). First, an "off-season" where you decide if you want to play (I mean work) and where. For me, I reassess what I do every summer – that's my "off- season". That doesn't mean I take the summer off. It means I make a conscious attempt to really think about how I want to spend the next season (I mean year).

Then, "training camp" starts – this is where you take the goals you've set during the "off-season" and start testing them out, putting them into practice, making the changes that are important to keep you vital and involved in what you do and acquiring the skills needed to succeed. After "training camp", comes the "regular season". These eight or nine months are where you knuckle down and do all you can to accomplish your goals and the goals you've agreed to deliver for your employer. But save some time for the "playoffs" (you know I mean the grand finale). This is the last minute push to get to your goals. Can you see why you will be looking forward to the "off-season" again? When you look at your career the way a sports player and his or her agent looks at how to use their talents, you are adapting to the new age. Shorter stays at many different companies. There are risks to looking at a career on a year-to-year basis, but in my experience there are more rewards than problems.

You may be asking yourself, sports figures sometimes sign long-term contracts. If the circumstances occur that you've got that kind of fit with a company, then why not? But keep in mind the four seasons of your work year and you'll have less burnout and more fulfillment.

To avoid digging yourself into a rut, plan your life one year at a time.

Rule #2 – Never Resign Over a Personality Conflict.

Years ago I heard a work psychologist interviewed on the radio. I forget her name, the program, the station – everything but what she said, which was – never let a personality conflict with an associate or a supervisor force you to quit the job you really like. I was taken aback by that because when someone wants to make you miserable you want to find work elsewhere. But this workplace author said wait it out if you really like your job. Good jobs are hard to find. Spend your time taking a human relations course or read some books on how to deal with difficult people. Why? Because more often than not if you hold on to the job you like, the company will eventually part ways with the person who you don't like.

Rule #3 – Work for Less at the Right Job.

I know what you're thinking. Some of my USC students wanted to land a $60,000 plus position right out of college. Some may. Many just want to find the right fit and get on with their careers. My advice has been and still is – take the lowliest, poorest paying job in the field of your choice rather than a better paying job somewhere else. You've heard all those stories about successful people who started in the mailroom. Do you know what it is about a mailroom that makes these people go on to success and riches? That mailroom is in the company they want to work for in the industry for which they have a passion. And yes, I've heard the answer, "But, Professor Del Colliano, I need the money to pay for my student loans", to which I usually answer, "Take a second job". Start at the bottom if you must in the right job if you want to succeed.

Rule #4 – "Seven Ways" to Get the Job of Your Dreams.

Well, here it is. The strategy that almost always works – time tested with young and hungry college students, lean on experience but chomping at the bit to start their careers.

The best favor you could do for your career is to de-emphasize "resume thinking". Job seekers are taught to toil over their resumes. My strategy is to do a one-page resume – cleanly edited, honest, descriptive, devoid of boasts that future employers do not believe in any case. In its stead, draw up a one-page Word document that lists "Seven Ways" Jane Doe Can Contribute to Apple, for example. My students would say, "Does it have to be seven ways?" I would answer, "Yes, of course, seven is a lucky number. People love it."

Number the seven items starting with #1. All statements of how you can specifically contribute to the company with which you are seeking employment. Caution: do not be tempted to use the same seven items with each prospective employer. The idea is to customize the ways your skills may fit with a specific company where you are seeking employment. One student called me on my cell phone in a panic after he got past number two, his second way to contribute to the company where he wanted to work. I asked what was wrong. He said he was having trouble coming up with the "Seven Ways". Ah, the advantages of disadvantages strikes again. He realized that this was not a job he should apply for. Instead, he found another prospect, did the "Seven Ways" and got the job. When preparing the page, each statement is followed by one more sentence that gives evidence to back up the assertion. For example, if you say, "Bring excellent human relations skills to collaborative situations" then the next line must be a real example of how you've done that. This gives you credibility and does not constitute a brag. Remember, one page. Seven assertions and seven sentences with evidence.

If you get to present the "Seven Ways" in person at an interview, walk in, look the interviewer in the eye, smile and firmly shake his or her hand. You ask the first question (and only one, please) to the interviewer about them, how they got their job, or how long they've worked for the company, then settle back and answer all questions honestly.

At the right point – you'll know when – say, "I have taken the liberty to prepare a list of ways I believe I could contribute to Ajax Communications. May I share them with you?" Because you will only carry one copy of the "Seven Ways" into the interview, put it in front of you for reference only and say in your own words what is on the paper. This should not exceed two minutes.

Before you leave, hand that sheet to your interviewer and you will have likely gone to the head of their list. "Seven Ways" you can contribute with evidence makes you a contender. At the end of the interview, stand and thank the employer for their time. Do not say, "I hope I hear from you" or other forms of groveling. Then, send a thank you with a similar sentiment within 24 hours.

Rule #5 – Remember the Ted Williams Rule.

If Ted Williams, one of the best baseball hitters ever, could bat .400 once in his career, we can't expect to bat a thousand on every interview. Achieving success four out of ten times means failing 60% of the time. Failure is good if you don't make it permanent. Learn from what you may have done wrong or what may have been wrong about the situation. Never get discouraged. *Never*. Good comes from bad even if you don't believe it so help it naturally occur by never giving up.

I was out of work for almost two years early in my career. I thought I would never work again. Some bad breaks and unfortunate people threw my career into chaos. I've suffered the humiliation of the unemployment line. Things have not always been good for me. So when I write about career chaos I must add that I wish that more people would have reassured me that I was going to be alright and someday be a success.

To paraphrase Bob Dylan, come to learn that career "chaos is a friend of mine".

11

DIVORCE

I always thought divorce was when two people could not get along with each other.

But I was wrong. It is actually the other way around. Divorce is when two people cannot get along with *themselves* and that's where all the trouble begins for them, their partner and the unsuspecting children of their union.

I ought to know. I have been married three times. My friend Father Martin Padovani, a priest counselor, asked me to address divorce in this book because as he put it, "You're an expert on this subject." I have a son, Jerry, from my first marriage and a daughter, Daria, from the second. They are everything to me. I cannot imagine what life would have been for me without them. I'll talk more about the children of divorce in a moment but first I'd like to address the heart of the problem from the perspective of a thrice-married man – very happily at last.

Divorce makes us fodder for jokes. "Which ex are you talking about?" I would hear with a giggle. The comedian Robin Williams was funnier, *"Ah, yes, divorce ... From the Latin word meaning to rip out a man's genitals through his wallet."* The multi-married Zsa Zsa Gabor used to say, *"I'm an excellent housekeeper. Every time I get a divorce, I keep the house."* It took Nirvana rocker Kurt Cobain to nail it, *"Mom hates dad, dad hates mom, it all makes you feel so sad."*

How is it that two people could be so in love as to actually memorialize their marriage in front of friends and family and then years later – sometimes just a few, sometimes many – they can barely find the flame that ignited their relationship in the first place? It happens all the time. We live in a society that openly expects the potential of divorce as an outcome. If you attend two weddings a year, you are within the statistical margin of error to expect that one of the two will eventually fail.

Another mitigating factor is that all the marriage counseling in the world doesn't seem to help a troubled couple because by the time most marriages get to the point where one or both of the partners are desperate enough to seek third-party intervention, it is usually too late. That is a sad but an accurate description of the sorry state of divorce. Father Padovani always reminded me that it may be too late for most marriages but it is just in time for each individual to save themselves *from themselves*. Because in the end, most of us marry out of emotion and/or need with very little attention to feelings and the ability to communicate. For example, if the Philadelphia Phillies baseball team chose its players by the way they looked or by some other emotion that made them feel good for the moment, they would never rightfully consider whether their partners could pitch, field and hit. Only in marriage do we tend to make emotional rather than rational decisions as adults.

So, revelation number 1 is – In divorce, you are actually divorcing yourself.

I knew a woman who married a chiropractor in Cherry Hill, NJ. He was cheating and she was onto it. Eventually, the marriage ended when both of them raced to the bank on Route 70 to get ahead of each other to close their account out. It was ugly. Maybe she never wanted to be married to a doctor and maybe the doctor never wanted to be married to a stay at home wife. But both sought the company of each other to try and complete that which they did not possess as individuals.

I once asked a friend of mine in the media business what it was like to be married a second time. He answered, "It's the same as the first marriage just different problems." I was taken aback but today I understand what he was saying. There is no getting around differences and personality conflicts but sooner or later you must commit to resolve them if you are to remain married. He did.

In high school, they teach health, science, math and the other subjects that are designed to give us what is called an education. But few schools teach human relations, principles of marriage, psychology and if they did, these topics might be too hot for some local communities. Yet, it is an undeniable fact, that marriage is the one thing for which most people have the least training – the highest expectations and the lowest ability. Our young students know how to play baseball or field hockey but know nothing about relationships. If they did, they would approach marriage more methodically because so much is at stake when a marriage fails.

Revelation 2 – A lack of self-love and self-esteem paves the way for divorce.

When something essential is lacking in one person, it becomes problematic in two. Divorce in many ways is the inability to love yourself. One needs to love oneself before loving another in a successful relationship. Many people look to marriage for the love of another, but if you study the good relationships, marriage has less to do with being loved than loving the other person. This is quite a revelation in therapy because like everything else in a world that has become increasingly self-absorbed, marriage is often defined as someone who loves *us* – not the other way around. Father Padovani writes, *"If we love ourselves we will take care and develop ourselves so we can reach out to others."*

He suggests that genuine self-love is not based on feeling but actions and sound reasoning – the opposite of what we might expect – or as he adds, *"It does not operate on feelings, impulse, or compulsion, all of which have no mind of their own."*

How can we be so sure that failed marriages result from not understanding the critical importance of self-love? Look no further than a divorcee who remarries. The Jewish Proverb sums it up, *"When two divorced people marry, four people get into bed."* You can't easily divorce the causes of divorce and they remain with all parties until they are resolved. Often, that second marriage fails. Does it fail because the next two individuals are bad people or does it fail because if we were better prepared, we wouldn't pick most of the people we marry out of a lineup? People often marry more than twice. That's what I did. I swore I would never marry again after the second time but I *did* because not only did the right person finally come along, the right Jerry actually showed up ready to love himself before he offered that love to another.

Revelation 3 – Two complete people make one complete marriage.

I had counseling – God knows, I have had counseling – after both of my divorces. And in a way it was the slow – *very* slow learning process for me – that began to bring changes to the way I thought and acted. Think for a second of a couple you know (maybe it is you and your partner) who has a good, loving and enduring marriage. You are likely to see two people who are not needy or at the very least are not *as* needy. I don't know how marriage counselors do their jobs. I'm glad I'm not in that business. They often have to endure two angry people who talk past each other and need to score debating points more than they need to connect, agree or at least come to an understanding about their differences.

What is really sad is that when two people can't get along, it is frequently because of things that have taken place in their lives *before* they met their partners and thus, the damage is being meted out to the person closest to them at the time (their spouse) instead of the person from their family of origin that helped them become so needy.

Revelation 4 – Most good marriages are made or broken well before they occur – in their families of origin.

That is why it is the lifelong pursuit of introspection that is the real journey of life. Opposites attract until they clash. Compatible couples proceed under the radar of divorce until they can no longer suppress their hostile feelings. In the end, it is a person happy with themselves, able to resolve any anger issues from childhood and willing to accept and improve their shortcomings who are the best candidates for marriage.

Once, before the age of contraception, women had their options impacted by fertility issues. Decades later, men and women seem to have proceeded no further than where they were mired previously. An unprecedented number of births out of wedlock even with many different ways available to manage this. Therefore, what used to be a big issue – the fertility question – is not as big but the issue of resolving individual problems from families of origin is now the elephant in the room of our counseling sessions.

Is marriage necessary? That's a good question. A clergyman might answer it one way and a lawyer might answer it another. So if you broaden the topic of divorce to include all meaningful relationships where the union fails, we're looking at an epidemic of the inability to get along with primarily *ourselves*.

What good can possibly come out of something as damaging as divorce? Even divorcees can attest to it if only to say, *"At least I got rid of him"*. Often, with time and introspection, we see the advantages of divorce as a means of resolving childhood issues that will surely plague us at every turn in our lives if it is left unresolved.

My daughter's mother met Father Padovani when he was speaking of relationships at a local New Jersey church during our separation. What did it mean to me to meet this man and face my own shortcomings? Wouldn't you say I owe my former wife for introducing me to him even if he couldn't save the relationship? Father Padovani's books

Healing Wounded Relationships and *Healing Wounded Emotions* should be required reading for everyone.

Revelation 5 – Counseling often saves individuals not marriages.

My son's mother gave me the gift of knowing in my heart of hearts that I wanted to devote my life to the broadcasting and media business. She may not have set out to become aware of this revelation, but she did after all was said and done. No degree of animosity, frustration or evil can alter the fact that out of bad marriages come good partners *for others* if they are willing to confront their shortcomings.

One of the tragedies of broken relationships is the adverse effect that they most always have on the children of these failed marriages. Children learn early the importance of words like "my lawyer" and "the judge" and "visitation". I always tried to turn the time I had with my children into something positive and happy. It wasn't always possible because I also know the meaning of those three terms. Yet, one very nice family counselor advised me on how to visit with my children after separation. I'd like to share it with you because it set the tone for what worked for my children and me. She said, *"Just show up when you are supposed to. Never cancel. If you must change your visit, add an extra one. Don't put on a show, simply make the child part of your daily living."* I took this to heart. I may have been a wreck. Tormented by my lawyer, the courts or the ex, but I always showed up.

My son, Jerry, and I got close because we had an hour drive in each direction on the days when we could see each other. That's four hours a day in a car (for me, two for him) and Jerry will tell you what he has often told me that the time we spent in that car in rain, sleet and snow (remember, we're talking Philadelphia here) are some of his fondest memories. Imagine that, just showing up and spending time.

My daughter, Daria, and I played and watched movies. I read her books and told her stories. It was our time and we made the best of it.

Both of my children began their love of ice hockey and particularly their love of the Philadelphia Flyers before they were six months old watching the game at the arena from the vantage point of dad's lap. My son's love of golf developed because we took it up together.

Divorce is such a major earthquake in our lives. It shakes up our beliefs, makes us suspicious and non-trusting, provides enough hurt and pain for everyone affected and yet it is such a gift when it happens. Don't get me wrong, I'd rather have gotten it right from day one if I could have. But I would never not want to be the father of my children and I now recognize that my exes are good people. That we all have our families of origin to work with and overcome and they do as well.

I can prove it.

As I look into the eyes of my children I see me but I also see their mothers and together we created the most beautiful product of our time together. And now I have come to learn – as I hope you will as well – that two good people aren't always right for each other until they are right for themselves and that what shaped us in childhood often impacts our ability to live in harmony with our chosen mates.

Today, my wife Cheryl is the love of my life because she is kind and understanding. I am also a different man today than I was previously. Therefore, had I not dealt with my issues acquired through childhood, I might not have been ready to take advantage of the opportunity she presented to have a great and healthy marriage.

That is why I thank those who helped me realize the advantages of disadvantages in divorce – and just in time for a chance at happily ever after.

Helen Rowland put it in a powerful way: *"When two people decide to get a divorce, it isn't a sign that they 'don't understand' one another, but a sign that they have, at last, begun to."*

I would add – begun to understand *themselves*.

Out of bad marriages come good people who, when they commit to dealing with their family of origin issues, can then enter into healthy relationships.

12

FINDING YOUR HIGHER POWER

"Without faith a man can do nothing, with it all things are possible." – Sir William Osler

By now perhaps you can see that whatever life throws at us, we can handle, but the glue that keeps us hoping and coping is faith.

Faith is not something reserved for the very religious as even Mother Teresa who is being considered for sainthood in the Catholic Church spent a lifetime of doubts as she worked to help the poor, the downtrodden, and the discarded souls in India. A biography entitled *Come Be My Light* features the letters she wrote to her church superiors as early as 1946 when she began her work among the poor. For the last 50 years of her life, we come to learn, Mother Teresa confessed to being unable to feel God's existence according to the account by Brian Kolodiejchuk.

Here is how this pious woman described her search for faith:

"I call, I cling, I want – and there is no One to answer – no One on Whom I can cling – no, No One. – Alone ... Where is my Faith – even deep down right in there is nothing, but emptiness & darkness – My God – how painful is this unknown pain – I have no Faith – I dare not utter the words & thoughts that crowd in my heart – & make me suffer untold agony.

"So many unanswered questions live within me afraid to uncover them – because of the blasphemy – If there be God – please forgive me – When I try to raise my thoughts to Heaven – there is such convicting emptiness that those very thoughts return like sharp knives & hurt my very soul. – I am told God loves me – and yet the reality of darkness & coldness & emptiness is so great that nothing touches my soul."

Mother Teresa's crisis of faith is far from scandalous. On the contrary, it shows how even religious people of great zeal and boundless energy are – well, human.

After all, faith eludes us especially in our modern world.

And yet, living requires faith. We humans have to believe in ourselves, in others when they earn it and in some Higher Power – whatever we call it – that gives us the strength to let go of our problems, disappointments and shortcomings so that we might overcome them.

Mother Teresa's inability to connect with her faith is actually very empowering to the rest of us. That is, we do not need to be saintly or religious or for that matter pious to seek the ability to believe in ourselves, others and our lives – whatever we wish for them. After all who is God? What is God? Is there a God? These are all questions that we must answer for ourselves in our own way, in our own time. But what is undeniable to me is that without faith in some Higher Power, it is not possible to transcend life's disappointments, hurts and adversity. I am not a man of the cloth – not a preacher. It is not my mission. Respectfully, I leave these questions for you to answer.

Belief that there is a Higher Power – a person or force that we can turn to in an attempt to believe in ourselves and let go of our problems – is critical. All my life I have tried to achieve the faith of others who seemingly never question the existence of God. Yet today, as imperfect as I know I am, I feel a stronger if not imperfect faith that I am not alone – ever. God works on the human condition. He is on our side, by our side and always forgives us. That's what I believe. It wasn't always that way for me. It isn't easy to let the shortcomings of organized religion taint the way we look at our faith.

Additionally, I always saw suffering as being the unfortunate byproduct of bad luck. Let me be very clear. I wouldn't choose suffering as a way to happiness but oddly enough it often turns out that way. And consistent with the theme of this book, then, even suffering is not off limits to becoming an advantage of a disadvantageous situation. Followers of Christ believe that suffering is not meaningless and it is redemptive. His suffering on the cross was totally unfair. Suffering has purpose. There is meaning to it and it is redemptive.

Even though there is misery all around us and problems that need to be solved, we can still be happy inside for happiness comes from within not from other people and the strength to believe it and achieve it comes from some sort of faith that we are not alone. Do the best you can and put it in God's hands – this is the most powerful prayer. There is no need to be pillars of piety. After all, it was Mother Teresa who said in the long run God isn't going to ask if you succeed or fail, but if you keep trying.

There are nine steps to getting in touch with the faith that we have in a Higher Power no matter how disconnected we may feel:

1. Take the gifts and resources that you have and develop them to become the person you are meant to be.

2. Cultivate a belief that whatever comes up, you can handle it. Believers say, with God you can get through it.

3. Differentiate between solving every problem that occurs and dealing with them one by one – this inner faith allows individuals to discover how powerful they can feel when they let go of the misfortune, irritations and suffering that comes their way. Instead, the mission is to substitute the need to solve every problem for simply dealing with them. All of us can succeed at dealing with problems. Solving them is an added benefit, not a prerequisite.

4. Spirituality is the real surrender. To let go of the suffering that plagues us will eventually require faith in something – some one – some force of nature. The inability to let go keeps us saddled with life's unfortunate circumstances. The moment you can offer it up to a Higher Power is the time when the burden gets lifted. No need to call this process anything other than – letting go. Religious people add, "and let God".

5. Become sensitive to the concept that suffering and sacrifice are strongly linked together. This is true in marriage, families and overcoming personal as well as health problems.

6. When you are ready or whether you are at wits end and can stand no more, surrender to your Higher Power, an act of ultimate spirituality. I have a friend who tells me he lays in bed at night and before he closes his eyes he let's go of his problems, frustrations, disappointments and pain as he relaxes his muscles. The mere act of physically relaxing while mentally lifting the burden of pain and suffering

allows him to get a good night's sleep the better to return to reality refreshed and ready to deal with life's problems.

7. Make time to think, be silent and have space and time for prayer. This is near impossible in our digital world where we are connected through cell phones and the Internet all day but where we ultimately must seek quiet to process our digital lives in a more analog way.

8. Life happens at increasingly faster speeds requiring us to seek balance, but it is no different than 50 years ago. Seeking balance in life has always been a challenge. No one's life is perfectly balanced, but a sense of trying to make it more balanced is necessary. When all we can have faith in is that our mobile carrier will keep Blackberry or Apple phone service up and running, we can appreciate how important a time-out can be to get connected to our souls.

9. Just be open to your Higher Power every day. Say "yes" to it in the morning because you never know what is going to come down the pike.

Author and psychologist Susan Jeffers book is called *Feel the Fear and Do It Anyway.* Transcend life's problems by seeking faith in a Higher Power. Develop the good to get beyond the past. Remarkably, we discover that as sure as life is full of problems, disappointments and challenges, we come to appreciate the advantages of disadvantages. They transform us even if the suffering that results cannot "solve" our problems or make them go away.

Things turn out when they are turned over to a Higher Power. It gives us personal power to deal with life's hurts and it is cheaper than an antidepressant or sleeping pill.

M. Scott Peck says, *"The truth is that our finest moments are most likely to occur when we are feeling deeply uncomfortable, unhappy or unfulfilled. For it is only in such moments, propelled by our discomfort, that we are likely to step out of our ruts and start searching for different ways or truer answers."*

Reach for a Higher Power when your faith is low.

13

THE BAD/GOOD
GAME PLAN

It's not the end of life if you are constantly hit with problems.

It *is* life.

The best way to make good out of bad is to face your problems whether they are deserved or not and deal with them straight on. A swimmer doesn't get to the other side of the pool unless she dives in and keeps paddling until she reaches her destination. To stop or falter in the middle of the pool would be tantamount to treading water just to stay afloat. That's a good analogy for what happens to us when we get overwhelmed with life's problems. We feel lucky to stay afloat even if it means going nowhere. But a change in perspective can retrain us to see adversity as a real opportunity. Face it. Deal with it. Keep going until you work through it.

Often when we readily decide to change – to make improvements in our lives or the way we live our lives – we become discouraged and give up. After all, years of reacting to bad luck, mean people and unfortunate events often makes us the victim of circumstances. Even when we want to make changes and adjust our attitude to be more positive, we fall short. It is as if we set out to travel to a destination that we can see clearly in our minds eye yet our arrival seems to never come.

One way I try to focus like a laser on that which I want to accomplish is to come up with a game plan for turning disadvantages into advantages.

To do that, we must work a specific program to actually look forward to the next problem or roadblock that gets in our way. That's right – look forward to your next problem. I can say this without sounding like a Pollyanna because the next problem and the ones after that will come your way in any case. But to look forward to handling it (notice I didn't say enjoying it) means that you know that eventually, if handled with the right attitude and approach, good will come out of bad. Just as the love of your life may only arrive after a divorce. Or as the loss of a friendship changes you in a way that makes you a better person. Or the loss of a job eventually paves the way for a new career, new opportunity and new prosperity.

So here it is – the Bad/Good Game Plan that you can work to accept the inevitable in a way that facilitates and even shortens the time in which you get the benefit.

Step 1 – Soak up every problem that comes your way with the attitude that you can handle it.

When a ballplayer stands in the outfield, he doesn't say to himself please *don't* hit the ball to me. He says the opposite – "Please send it my way. I can handle it." And most of the time a ballplayer does handle it and so *we* can handle whatever comes our way. It's coming anyway, so why not confidently say – I can handle it. You'll also note that whenever a ballplayer makes an error, a mistake whether costly to his team or not he shows us what *we* need to do when we make a mistake in handling our problems. "Hit it to me again" – that's the mantra. If ballplayers crave the opportunity to play their game, why can't we crave the opportunity to deal with our lives? More often than not, we'll handle what comes our way. But sometimes we cannot. And that's where we need to cultivate the yearning for another shot at it. Once we are able to say "bring it on" to the ups and downs in our daily lives without the mandate that everything works out well, then we can move on to the next step.

Step 2 – Deal with your problems.

As I've said previously, some problems go away by themselves. Others, we can fix. And *some* we have to accept because their circumstances cannot be changed (as in the death of a loved one or the loss of a career opportunity). Here is a simple thought to keep in mind. Your job is to accept that which happens to you and spend more productive time determining which problems can be solved, which cannot and knowing the ones that must be accepted. Go to work and try to deal with each and every one of them over time. When you are divorcing, you cannot make that process, as painful as it often is, go away in a day or with one strategy. Time is required because it is specifically time that is the underappreciated catalyst for turning bad into good.

Step 3 – Move on.

Too frequently life's problems get us down. They alter the course of our lives without our consent, but only if we deal with these problems in the proactive way I've described, can we avoid wallowing in them. I'm sure you can join me in not taking too long to remember the last time you hung onto a problem or negative circumstance longer than necessary. Sometimes we even suffer mental paralysis even after we've dealt with a problem successfully but have not let it go. Deal with it and move on – that's our new goal from now on.

Step 4 – Seek help from a Higher Power.

Whether it is God or some other expression of spirituality that is best suited to you, the burden of pain that life can sometimes inflict is more adequately dealt with when we can let go and put some of the burden into the realm of a Higher Power. For those who believe in God, God is your friend who is on your side, by your side and who never lets you down. That's what I like to say when I am overburdened and in over my head. A more abstract expression of a Higher Power can also give you a break from life's burdens we are often asked to carry. Without a Higher Power to turn to, it can become difficult to cope with the disadvantages that come our way – even if we can believe that something good or even great can eventually result from it.

Step 5 – Cultivate an "Attitude of Gratitude".

That's a great term used by the psychologist Father Martin Padovani to accentuate the need to always be on the lookout for that which is good in our lives. The reasoning may be obvious but the act of searching for things for which to be grateful isn't always easy. Why? Because they are often right before our eyes – the simple things that we have conditioned ourselves to expect and not appreciate. The advantages of the flu over terminal cancer is that the flu lasts a week or less and almost always leads to full recovery. Do you know anyone who can be grateful for getting the flu and not terminal cancer? See, that's what I mean. An "attitude of gratitude" is an ongoing process that must occur in real-time and not philosophically after the fact. The reason you'll like ramping up being more grateful for that which is right in your life is because it makes you feel good – kind of a mood elevator without a prescription and it sustains you when dealing with various types of problems that often and temporarily put us at a disadvantage.

So, there you have it. Five steps that require change – change that can make you happier and provide you with the sustenance to handle almost anything that comes your way.

Every morning, as I look into the mirror and shave, I set the compass for my day. What kind of a person am I, I ask. What kind of a person do I want to be? What is worrying me? How can I focus on dealing with whatever life has put on my plate? Do I like the person I am looking at in the mirror? Can I think fondly or pray for those who bring joy to my life? Am I big enough to pray for those who have done evil to me and others – it is healing to do so and releases the vitriol that could work against me. You can spend some time at the start of each day setting your attitude so that when you step out you are ready for the world as it is – for better or for worse.

There is little advantage to looking back on something that has happened to you years ago and commenting that it all worked out for the best. That's history. And unfortunately, you know what happens to history. It repeats itself.

But when you can get to the point where when all hell is breaking loose with bad breaks, disappointment, broken promises and relationships to be able to say, *"Something good is going to come out of this. I don't know how. I don't know where. I don't when, but I know it will."*

Once that is your reaction to the bad that we must suffer through to live life, you've unlocked the secret. You've become a better roller coaster rider. A more confident problem solver. A more grateful human being.

I never expected to be married three times when I participated in the first ceremony, but it was worth waiting for.

That a career teaching young people is nothing I would have ever aspired to when all I could taste and smell was radio and television broadcasting, but it was the most rewarding.

My two children gave me the honor of being their father – divorce was not a deterrent, it just heightened how special we are to each other.

I've been fired, unemployed, this close to losing my house and never could I have seen that these "gifts" made me more determined to succeed in my career – an edge that someone with that "advantage" could never have known.

For it is that no human is omniscient enough to see into the future. No person knows for sure what he or she wants in the future or even what is necessarily best for us.

That is also life.

When things get you down, now you have a way to look up. Pick up the cross and carry it. The good will happen *anyway*. For as sure as the sun will rise tomorrow, out of bad comes good and you will eventually be the beneficiary of the advantages of life's disadvantages.

Good happens anyway. Be prepared.

ABOUT THE AUTHOR

Jerry Del Colliano is a nationally recognized expert on broadcasting, journalism, interactive and social media content. His on-air and executive experience spans television, radio, publishing and new media. Jerry's interest in transformational self-improvement comes from his 11 years as a Dale Carnegie instructor and college professor.

He was appointed Clinical Professor at the University of Southern California in 2004 where he developed and taught classes in music industry, generational and new media as well as collaborative courses in communications.

Jerry has been interviewed as a media expert on network television and has been quoted in hundreds of publications as diverse as *The New York Times* and *Washington Post* to *People Magazine* and *Rolling Stone*.

Today, Jerry teaches the advantages of disadvantages in inspirational presentations and business seminars to help diverse groups of people unlock the power of turning misfortune into good fortune.

Out of Bad Comes Good – The Advantages of Disadvantages is ignited by the next generation and is about today's human condition and how to find success and happiness as well as overcome problems in a changing world. Once we learn to anticipate, recognize and deal with adversity, the author believes it can become a powerful force in our lives.

INTERESTED IN HAVING
JERRY DEL COLLIANO
SPEAK AT YOUR NEXT EVENT?

Jerry's motto is "the teacher and the taught together do the teaching" and people who have heard him speak or worked with him in business brainstorming sessions have discovered that through mistakes – *real growth can happen!*

Jerry shows you with his own inspirational stories and specific tools on how to learn from adversity.

He teaches leaders and their team members the importance of finding success in setbacks. And motivates audiences of all kinds to learn to appreciate the advantages of disadvantages as they occur in their daily lives. Jerry believes in new age solutions to the challenging and changing human condition.

If your company has a challenging road ahead or faces increased competition in your industry, Jerry Del Colliano can give you the tools to be better, stronger and smarter to stay on top or move ahead.

Out of Bad Comes Good – The Advantages of Disadvantages is an attainable and successful way of life.

To unlock the human potential that all of us have through hard knocks, bad breaks, and life's ups and downs, you must hear Jerry in person.

If you are interested in having Jerry speak at your next event or company meeting, please contact Bobi Seredich at <u>bobi@eqspeakers.com</u> or Jerry Del Colliano at <u>jdelcolliano@earthlink.net</u>.

BUY A SHARE OF THE FUTURE IN YOUR COMMUNITY

These certificates make great holiday, graduation and birthday gifts that can be personalized with the recipient's name. The cost of one S.H.A.R.E. or one square foot is $54.17. The personalized certificate is suitable for framing and will state the number of shares purchased and the amount of each share, as well as the recipient's name. The home that you participate in "building" will last for many years and will continue to grow in value.

Here is a sample SHARE certificate:

HABITAT FOR HUMANITY

THIS CERTIFIES THAT

__YOUR NAME HERE__

HAS INVESTED IN A HOME FOR A DESERVING FAMILY

1985-2010

TWENTY-FIVE YEARS OF BUILDING FUTURES
IN OUR COMMUNITY ONE HOME AT A TIME

1200 SQUARE FOOT HOUSE at $65,000 = $54.17 PER SQUARE FOOT
This certificate represents a tax deductible donation. It has no cash value.

YES, I WOULD LIKE TO HELP!

I support the work that Habitat for Humanity does and I want to be part of the excitement! As a donor, I will receive periodic updates on your construction activities but, more importantly, I know my gift will help a family in our community realize the dream of homeownership. **I would like to SHARE in your efforts against substandard housing in my community!** *(Please print below)*

PLEASE SEND ME _____ SHARES at $54.17 EACH = S $_____

In Honor Of: _____

Occasion: (Circle One)   HOLIDAY   BIRTHDAY   ANNIVERSARY

    OTHER: _____

Address of Recipient: _____

Gift From: _____   *Donor Address:* _____

Donor Email: _____

I AM ENCLOSING A CHECK FOR $ $_____ PAYABLE TO HABITAT FOR HUMANITY **OR** PLEASE CHARGE MY VISA OR MASTERCARD *(CIRCLE ONE)*

Card Number _____ Expiration Date: _____

Name as it appears on Credit Card _____ Charge Amount $ _____

Signature _____

Billing Address _____

Telephone # Day _____ Eve _____

PLEASE NOTE: Your contribution is tax-deductible to the fullest extent allowed by law.
Habitat for Humanity • P.O. Box 1443 • Newport News, VA 23601 • 757-596-5553
www.HelpHabitatforHumanity.org

9 781614 480167